Exploring Feelings

Discussion Book

for

Gifted Kids Have Feelings Too

Sylvia B. Rimm

Christine E. Priest

Library of Congress Cataloging in Publication Data

Rimm, Sylvia B.
Exploring Feelings: discussion book for
Gifted Kids Have Feelings Too

Bibliography: p. 110
1. Education 2. Psychology
3. Gifted 4. Adolescence

W6050 Apple Road, Watertown, Wisconsin 53094
(414) 261-1118 FAX (414) 261-6622

Printed and bound in the United States of America.

ISBN No. 0-937891-07-X
Library of Congress Catalog Card No. 90-082399

Dedicated to the caring parents and teachers who share the stresses and the joys of guiding adolescents toward a fulfilling adult life.

TABLE OF CONTENTS

PREFACE

Gifted Kids Have Feelings Too was developed with a concern for the social and emotional needs of teenagers. The stories can be read for general interest and thinking or they can be used for group discussion and activities. They are targeted at teenagers' experiences. This parent and teacher discussion book, *Exploring Feelings*, provides suggested questions and curriculum activities for individual students, groups or classes. The students' ages, interests or specific concerns should serve to guide teachers and parents in their selection of particular activities or discussion questions.

The main themes of the stories include anti-intellectual peer pressure, coping with competition, relationships with parents, siblings and friends, competition, underachievement, independence, loneliness, goal setting, peer social life issues, and grade acceleration. *Exploring Feelings* includes suggestions for many interpretations of stories. You and/or your adolescents may also want to select or create other discussion topics or activities.

GIFTED KIDS HAVE FEELINGS TOO

DISCUSSION QUESTIONS

1. What do the kids call students who have excellent grades in your school? Are these references to excellent students negative, positive, neutral or do they differ depending on the student?

2. Is peer pressure different if the "brainy" student is male or female? Are there any other characteristics of the student that seem to cause the "brainy" label to be negative or positive?

3. Have you ever been labeled a "brain" by other students? If so, how did you feel?

4. If kids are known as "brains," do you think it motivates them to study harder or do you think it puts pressure on them not to study as much?

5. Did you ever do poorly on a test because you didn't want a reputation for being brainy? Do you know anyone who ever did? How do you feel about deliberately doing less well on a test?

6. Do you think that there is peer pressure to not appear too smart? How does that peer pressure take place and how does it differ in different grades of school?

7. Do you feel any peer pressure to get higher grades or to study harder?

8. Do you know students in other schools who have experienced other peer pressures for avoiding studying or for studying too hard?

9. Are "brainy" kids ever also popular students? Is popularity important? Read *Popularity Ends at Grade 12* (Rimm, 1988) and *Is Popularity Worth Pursuing?* (Rimm, 1987c) and discuss again.

10. Are "brainy" students respected by most other students? What are the characteristics which gain student respect?

11. What part does jealousy play in the peer pressure that "brainy" kids may feel?

12. Do you think Maria could have been more helpful to Sally? What would you have said or done if you had been Maria?

13. Read "*Why Do Bright Children Underachieve? The Pressures They Feel* (Rimm, 1987b). Do you think pressure referred to in this article contributes to students' responses to peer pressure?

14. Do you ever feel peer pressure to achieve and peer pressure to underachieve? How do these contradictory pressures affect you or others that you know?

PROJECTS AND ACTIVITIES

Interviewing

Interview your parents or grandparents about peer pressure they felt when they were in middle or high school. Ask them what "brainy" kids were called in their generation and about what happened to those "brainy" kids after they left high school. Tape-record their responses and bring them in to share with your class. Then compile a list of labels that have been used for "brainy" kids in middle or high school in the past. Are there cultural or time differences that affect peer pressures on highly intelligent adolescents? Discuss these differences.

Creative Writing

1. Rewrite Sally's story as if she had given in to peer pressure and decided that school wasn't worth her effort. Imagine how her parents, siblings and peers would have responded to Sally as a poor student who stopped doing homework. Imagine how Sally would have felt about herself. Share your story with the class.

2. Pretend you are Sally's parents or brothers or Sally's friend, Maria. Rewrite the story from their point of view changing it to reflect your impression of Sally and of what you would say or do for Sally. Feel free to add or change characters.

3. Michael Wendt, a teacher of English and history at Lakeridge High School in Lake Oswego, Oregon, has created an 11-line poem called a "*Bio-Poem.*"*

This is the form that the poem should follow:

Line 1:	Your first formal, second formal name
Line 2:	(Sibling of ...) List names of brothers and sisters (or daughter of, son of)
Line 3:	(Lover of ...) Finish this statement
Line 4:	(Most conscious of ...) Indicate one, two or three ideas that are important to you
Line 5:	(To whom happiness is ...) Finish this statement
Line 6:	Use four adjectives or adjective phrases that you might use to describe yourself (they should be complimentary)
Line 7:	(Hoping for ...) Finish this statement
Line 8:	(Enjoying the sounds of ...) Finish this statement
Line 9:	(Likes to wear ...) Finish this statement (tell what clothing do you feel most comfortable in)
Line 10:	(Resident of) City, street name
Line 11:	Use your last name

*Used with the permission of Michael Wendt

Write a bio-poem. How did writing this poem help you to be better in touch with yourself? Will others know you better?

Make up your own form for a poem including those items that would help you and others to understand you better. Write a poem using your own form.

Increasing Sensitivity

1. Interview three or four students in your school who are known as "brains." What questions would you like to ask these students? (Create an interview form to use that would gather the information you would like, keeping in mind the feelings of these students. Find out if they feel sadness or pressure. Be sure to keep their names confidential.

In class, brainstorm ways in which students can learn to cope with negative peer pressure and how your school can provide a more supportive environment for students who care a lot about learning.

2. A teacher can do a great deal to help a student to feel comfortable in the classroom. Studies have shown that when students feel secure, they are more likely to be creative, productive learners. Teachers can work to create a classroom environment based on security and trust. If Sally's teacher had been aware of the importance of the learning setting, she would not have announced Sally's grade to the whole class.

Brainstorm a list of things a teacher can do to help create a comfortable and secure environment.

Now without using teachers' names, make a list of things teachers have done that could have made you or others feel uncomfortable and insecure.

Make two similar lists for things that fellow students could do to help and to hurt the classroom environment.

3. Late elementary, middle school, or early high school can be some of the most difficult times to accept oneself and recognize one's own strengths and talents. It's a time when peer relationships can be a high priority for many young people. It's perfectly normal to have these feelings. Many students are uncomfortable calling attention to themselves or standing out or being different in any way. Knowing yourself can be a big help.

The book, *Please Understand Me: Character and Temperament Types*, by Dave Keirsey and Marilyn Bates (1978), uses an assessment based on the *Myers-Briggs Type Indicator* (Myers, Briggs, & Briggs, 1988, 1976) to help a person to better understand him/herself. Take this assessment.

What are some of the things that you already knew about yourself that were substantiated by the test? What new understandings do you now have? What would you like others to know about you? How can this help you to better appreciate yourself and others? How can you use this information to help you in your relationships with others?

Creative Drama

Divide into two groups to play a game of charades. Use the following words and any other similar words:

> *Nerd, geek, druggie, teacher's pet, brain, member of the "in" crowd, cheerleader, basketball star, loner, goody-goody, social deviant, playboy, class clown, skateboarder, normal, dirt-bag, jock, preppie, etc.*

Were these easy to act out? Which ones were easiest? Why do you think some were easy to guess? Why are stereotypes like these cruel and unfair?

Analysis of a Movie

View the movie, *Dead Poet's Society* (1989). In this movie, the talents and feelings of a gifted boy were misunderstood by his parents.

In *Gifted Kids Have Feelings Too* (Rimm, 1990), Sally was able to share some of her frustrations of being gifted and misunderstood with an older brother who had had similar experiences to Sally's. Why was this such a help to her in coping with her situation?

In the movie, the boy who played Robin Goodfellow (Puck) in the play did not share his feelings with his parents. If his parents had been able to understand him, how might this movie have been different?

After you have seen the movie, discuss the following questions:

1. Have you ever felt that you had no ownership in ideas or plans that your parents have made for you?
2. How do you feel about parental expectations?
3. Are you able to share your feelings with your parents?
4. Usually people are more motivated when they have input. Could you help them to understand your need to have some control over your life?
5. Thinking about the movie, why is it so important to learn to share your feelings with others?
6. What support were the members of the *Dead Poet's Society* able to provide for one another?
7. Why is it important for gifted kids to have an opportunity to spend some time with groups of other gifted kids?
8. How did having a teacher like Robin Williams make learning exciting?
9. What type of learning environment was he able to create?

THE GIFT

Lisa Lovance, Age 11

DISCUSSION QUESTIONS

1. Do you think that Lisa felt lonely or good about her individuality? Have you had similar feelings? Describe feelings of pressure which you may feel to be either similar or different from others.

2. How do you feel about other students who exhibit similar behaviors or fashions mainly because they are considered acceptable to their friends?

3. Does it take courage to be different? Does it take courage to be similar?

4. Why do you think that teenagers often dress or act in similar ways?

5. How do you feel about Lisa's use of the word, "perfect?" What are the advantages and disadvantages of feeling "perfect" or never feeling "perfect" enough?

6. What is the difference between "excellence" and "perfection?"

7. What are some possible interpretations of the title of this poem?

8. What are some of the difficulties associated with being an individual or being different? Begin with some of the ideas that Lisa reveals in the lines of her poem. Add other ideas that you have seen in your observations of others or that you may have experienced yourself.

9. What are some of the ways that people give or receive the message that it is important or desirable to conform?

PROJECTS AND ACTIVITIES

Creative Writing

Write a personal letter to Lisa to explain how you feel about the issues she's presented to you in her poem. Then share your letters with your class. Did you interpret Lisa's poem differently? Did you respond to her with different advice or explanations? What accounts for the differences and similarities in the responses?

Artistic Expression

Express Lisa's feelings in a visual art or musical art form. Share your artistic expressions with your class.

Research

One issue that is frequently discussed among those with an interest in giftedness is whether someone is born gifted, whether someone's giftedness is the product of his/her environment, or whether it is some combination of both. This is often referred to as the "trait-state" nature of giftedness or the "nature-nurture" controversy. These ideas are difficult to research, but studies have been done with identical twins who for some reason have been placed in different environments shortly after birth. Read some research studies in this genetic vs. environment debate and share with your class.

One possible explanation for the last six lines of the poem would be to look at "giftedness" as something that is there, that a person chooses to recognize and deal with or chooses to ignore. How can these last six lines be interpreted in this way? How could they be interpreted as a message about pressures to hide giftedness and to give in to pressure to be like everyone else? How does the research in the nature-nurture controversy help you to interpret the effects of peer pressures on giftedness?

THE BOY WHO WOULDN'T GO TO SCHOOL

DISCUSSION QUESTIONS

1. Have you ever felt so bored in a class that you believed you couldn't sit through the class? If so, what did you do under those circumstances?

2. What does the term "boring" mean to you and do you think the term is used by everyone in the same way? Brainstorm different meanings of the word "boring."

3. If Brad couldn't have left his school and you were Dr. Ryan, can you think of ways you might have helped him at his old school?

4. Are there students you know who seem "socially awkward," for example, just don't know how to talk to friends? If you had a friend who didn't know how to fit in with friends socially, what advice would you give him or her?

5. Do males or females seem to have more social problems at your school? Why do you think that's the case?

6. When a new student comes to your school, are they usually well accepted? If they are unusually intelligent, does that help or hinder their acceptance?

7. When Brad refused to go to school and did nothing but sit and watch TV, he was feeling depressed. What are the characteristics of depression? Have you ever felt depressed? What seems to help you get out of your depression?

8. Have you ever gone to visit a psychologist? How did you feel before your first visit -- worried, scared, enthusiastic or some other way? Did you find it helpful to work with the psychologist?

9. How would you feel if you were Brad's close friend, but had to take regular classes? Would Brad's special treatment seem unfair?

10. How would you feel about being Brad's girlfriend? Could you think of things to do and talk about with him?

PROJECTS AND ACTIVITIES

Role-Play

Pretend you are the principal and are talking to Brad. Try to convince Brad of a way he can function in school while being fair to other students who are required to take regular courses and do homework. Someone should play Brad's role and argue for his point of view as well.

Creative Problem Solving

1. At the point that the reader meets Brad in this story, Brad is very frustrated and desperate. What signs are there that this is how he feels?

Before Brad got to this point, he might have tried a process called *Creative Problem Solving* (Parnes, Noller, & Biondi, 1976). Use a creative problem solving approach to help Brad figure out some options for solving his educational problems.

a. Brainstorm possible problems.
b. Define an underlying problem: "In what ways might Brad . . . ?"
"How might Brad . . . ?"

c. Brainstorm possible solutions.
d. Create criteria for selection and evaluation.
e. Select and write-up the "best" solution.

2. Sometimes we find ourselves in situations that are less than ideal but that cannot be changed. At times like this, we need to find ways to cope with our situation. Suppose Brad had to stay at the first school and no changes could be made. Make a list of negative and positive responses that Brad might have had.

3. If you, like Brad, were able to create your own educational program, what would it be like? Describe the program and tell why you think it would be a good program for you. In creating the program, what did you need to know about yourself?

Even if you cannot create your own imaginary program, are there some changes you could make in your present one that you feel would make learning even more exciting for you? Who would you go to with your ideas? How do you think these people would react to your ideas?

4. Brainstorm all the different ways that students who learn faster than typical students could show competency in a course or could show initiative in completing curriculum requirements.

Increasing Sensitivity

One's point of view is often the basis for decisions that one makes. In order to better understand how the people who are playing important roles in Brad's educational experiences are reacting to Brad, make a web to show how you feel the following people "see" Brad: the principal of the first school; Brad's mother; Dr. Ryan, the psychologist; the new counselor; and Brad, himself.

Webs of How Different People View Brad

Brad's Point of View:

Misunderstood, logical, angry, frustrated, desperate, smart, bored, lonely, patient, socially awkward, rational, etc. Add more.

Mother's Point of View:

Resigned, multi-talented, alone, competent, discouraged, bored, gifted, good, misunderstood, intelligent, etc. Add others.

Psychologist's Point of View:

Uncompromising, self-aware, angry, gifted, withdrawn, insightful, discouraged, socially insecure, underachieving, depressed, etc.

Principal's Point of View:

Lazy, stubborn, defiant, immature, nonconforming, persistent, obnoxious, demanding, rebellious, opinionated, rigid, bright, etc.

New Counselor's Point of View:

Someone with special needs, a professional challenge, gifted, an independent learner, self-motivated, determined, someone with different learning styles, etc.

1. After completing the webs, how do you think each of the people could have benefitted from seeing the webs you have created?

2. If Brad had been able to remove himself from the situation and look at these webs, how might he have approached the first principal differently?

3. Predict what might have been different if Brad's mother's perception of Brad had been different.

4. Predict a different outcome if the psychologist's point of view had been different.

5. Predict the outcome if the counselor had not been creative and flexible.

Learning to Compromise

Brad was unwilling to compromise about learning Shakespeare. Do you feel he was being reasonable? Why was he later willing to compromise and study English?

Brad was unwilling to compromise his belief that he could study his math more effectively by working independently in his own learning style. Do you feel Brad was correct?

How does one decide when to and when not to compromise? Learning to compromise is not always easy to do. Are there some things that you would easily compromise? Make a list of those things.

Are there some things that you would find difficult to compromise? Make a list of these.

Compare your two lists. What have you discovered about yourself? Do you find compromising is:

No problem at all
Very easy to do
Fairly easy to do
Fairly difficult to do
Very difficult to do
Almost impossible?

Are there issues where your willingness to compromise or not, differ from your classmates? What are the advantages and disadvantages of attitudes toward compromise?

Creative Writing

1. Sometimes it is difficult to break mind-sets. While the reader doesn't really get to know the counselor very well, by his actions one can make some assumptions about the type of person who would be willing to make these changes for Brad. Make a list of possible attributes of the new counselor. When you have completed your list, write a paragraph describing the kind of person you picture the counselor to be.

2. People often find themselves in a position where something written becomes the selected method of communication. Perhaps it is the choice for an initial

contact, or perhaps it is a follow-up to a phone conversation or a conference. After completing the story, *The Boy Who Wouldn't Go To School*, select one of the following letters to write as your creative writing assignment:

1. Pretend that you are Brad's mother and that you are writing a letter to Dr. Ryan, Brad's psychologist, requesting that she accept Brad as a client. Your hope is that she can help Brad work through issues contributing to his school achievement difficulties.

2. Pretend that you are Brad and that you are writing to your original high school principal. You would like him to make some changes that would individualize your educational program.

3. Pretend that you are Dr.Ryan and that you are writing to the guidance counselor at Brad's new school. You are writing to request special programming based on your client's needs. Be sure to support your request with evidence from your meetings with Brad.

4. Pretend that you are Brad's mother and that you are writing to Dr. Ryan to report to her Brad's adjustment when he returned to his original school. What has pleased you about his progress and what are your continued concerns?

FAT, FAT, FAT

DISCUSSION QUESTIONS

1. Do you know anyone who has had an eating disorder -- bulimia or anorexia nervosa? Do you know what these eating disorders are? Why do you think there are increasing numbers of high school and college students who have eating disorders? Teenage males have fewer eating disorders. Why do you suppose eating disorders are less prevalent among males?

2. How important is appearance and thinness in the selection of your friends or of your dates?

3. What, if any, pressures have you felt to lose weight?

4. Should weight and appearance be considered in selecting students for drama parts?

5. Have you ever teased other teens or your siblings about being overweight? How do they respond? How would you respond if you were teased?

6. Have there been some teachers who have had major positive impacts on you or on some

friends you know, similar to the impact of Mr. Rodney on Marna? Describe and discuss the kinds of teachers who make major positive changes for students.

7. Are there other teenage experiences which pressure students toward unhealthy thinness such as popularity, fashion modeling, parent or peer pressure? Talk about how teenagers can assertively cope with these pressures and avoid eating disorders.

8. How could the emphasis on a beautiful, thin body contribute to eating disorders?

9. In what context have you heard about the illegal use of steroids? Might some of the same problems that contribute to eating disorders be associated with steroid use?

10. While this story may appear to be primarily a female struggle, what might be some comparable struggles males may experience relative to body image?

PROJECTS AND ACTIVITIES

Research

Analyze the height and weight of students in your class by gender (males and females separately) and make comparisons to health/weight standards for teenagers. What percentage are in the correct weight range, what percentage are underweight and what percentage are overweight? Are there regional, national, or racial implications for typical heights or weights in your school?

Health Plan

Design a healthful diet and an exercise program for an overweight teenager. Read books on teenage nutrition, interview a dietician or ask your family physician for help. Live according to the health plan for at least a week. Talk about your feelings and experiences with your class.

Creative Writing

Write a story or a poem from the perspective of a person with an eating problem.

Role-Play

Try to imagine the feelings of someone with an eating problem. Then try to imagine what people might say to help you most with your problem. Role-play a conversation between the person with the eating problem and a friend who wants to help.

Drama is an excellent vehicle for encouraging self-confidence in students. It also encourages creativity and provides a positive group activity for many students. Brainstorm ways in which more students in your school could have experiences with drama.

Creative Drama

Select or write a brief play. Cast the parts based on acting ability alone, selecting actors and actresses who least physically fit the parts (e.g., males for females, small people for adults, large people for children, etc.). Try to act the parts appropriately and discuss afterwards how the physical misfits affected the cast and the audience.

Increasing Sensitivity

Having control, giving control, and controlling can be both positive and negative. Brainstorm a list of examples of positive use of control. Now make a list of negative uses of control. Compare and contrast the two lists. Are there any on either list that someone could justify placing on the other list? How do people abuse control?

Early in the story, Marna did not have control over her eating. Give examples to support this. Later she did not need to control her eating. Why not?

Marna controlled and manipulated herself and others with her eating disorder. How did she do this? Who was she able to control?

Marna needed to learn not to use eating habits as a controlling device. In attempting to treat Marna, the hospital had to take Marna's ability to control away from her. In what ways did the hospital therapists try to do this?

Visual Analysis

Marna and many other young girls and women have gotten the message that being "thin and pretty" is a "highest priority." It is not difficult to see where they have gotten this message. Television and movie actresses are slim and trim, beautifully made-up and coiffured. Magazines show "thin and pretty" women in their advertising. Make a collage of "thin and pretty" pictures showing how Marna could get the idea that it is a "highest priority." Make a similar collage with a message often conveyed to adolescent boys and men. One such message might be that "muscular and athletic" is a high priority.

ideas

Andrew Rubinstein, Age 17

DISCUSSION QUESTIONS

1. Does Andy's visual imagery of ideas fit with how you feel when you are thinking creatively?

2. Do your ideas seem to move of their own volition sometimes, almost as if you don't control them or would you characterize your thinking as more managed and in control?

3. Do you find it helpful to use visual imagery to describe feelings? Do you understand yourself better as a result?

PROJECTS AND ACTIVITIES

Creative Writing

1. Are there differences in the imagery you could use for varied kinds of thinking, learning and creating? Could you characterize by analogy the varieties of thinking you use? Develop your own analogies individually and then share them with your class. Did other students use similar analogies to yours? Do others think in similar or different ways than you? Discuss the reasons for the similarities and differences.

2. Write a poem to describe your feelings when you are thinking creatively.

the enemy separated us

Andrew Rubinstein, Age 17

DISCUSSION QUESTIONS

1. Have you ever had a very close friendship in which your friend was no longer interested in continuing the relationship? How did that feel? What could you do?

2. Have you ever had a close friend who shared your values and then suddenly became involved in heavy drinking or drugs? Does Andy's poem express feelings similar to those you experienced? Were you sad, depressed or angry? Was there any way that you found you could reach your friend to convince him/her that there was a problem?

3. What would you do if a close friend became heavily involved in drugs and he/she was at serious risk?

PROJECTS AND ACTIVITIES

Creative Writing

Why might young people suddenly leave close long-time friendships? Brainstorm many reasons why friendships may break up. Write a story or poem about a friendship which has broken up from the point of view of the friend who breaks up or from the point of view of the person rejected or left behind. You may want to write companion poems or stories that reflect the feelings of both.

IT'S DUMB TO BE SMART

and

HE'S NOTHING BUT A CHEAT

(Companion Stories)

DISCUSSION QUESTIONS

1. What do you think of Jennie's "Don't List?" Are there any activities on the list that you avoid doing because of peer pressure? Do you know anyone that has told you that any of the "Don't List" activities have caused them peer pressure?

2. Some gifted kids use two sets of vocabularies -- one for friends and one for classes. Do you speak a different vocabulary with your friends than with adults or in class or do you know anyone who does? What's the effect on other teenagers of students who use a highly intellectualized vocabulary?

3. Jennie and Bob dealt with their loneliness in very different ways. Would you have suspected that

either felt lonely by their behaviors? What other ways do teenagers cope with feelings of loneliness? Do you think all people feel lonely sometimes?

4. If you knew Jennie or Bob, would you be willing to reach out to either of them and be a friend? What might have prevented you from choosing them as friends?

5. Do you know any very bright students who have achieved very well in school despite cultural or economic disadvantage? What do you think made a difference in helping them?

6. It's not uncommon for teachers to assume that students have copied excellent stories, poems or reports. How could you handle such an accusation in a way that would prove your innocence without embarrassing the teacher or yourself?

7. Do you think the story would have been different if Jennie's part was characterized by a male and Bob's by a female? Research indicates that males are more willing to consider themselves "brains" than are females. Do you find this gender bias in your school?

8. How else could the guidance counselor have helped Jennie and Bob, either separately or together? Brainstorm for other ideas.

9. Are there any Jennies or Bobs that need help in your school? Could you be of help to them? Talk about how you could help without mentioning specific names.

10. How do you think Jennie's parents and Bob's parents felt about how to help their children? What could they have done to be more helpful?

11. Mr. Jackson's idea of having Jennie and Bob meet and talk in his office turned out to be successful for Jennie. How does the reader know this to be true? Give some evidence that it may also have been beneficial for Bob.

12. In what ways are Bob's problems more severe than Jennie's? Did the severity of Bob's problems contribute to his solution not being as successful? Do you think Bob will solve his problems eventually?

PROJECTS AND ACTIVITIES

Creative Writing

1. Make up a personal set of **Dos** and **Don'ts** for intellectual integrity and personal independence. Will these rules cause you problems with your peers? If so, how can your school help you?

2. Write a realistic story about how Bob could resolve his problem in a positive and successful way.

3. Select a descriptive word for each letter of Jennie's name. Do this first from Jennie's point of view and then from Bob's. Select a descriptive word for each letter of Bob Johnson's name. Try this activity using your own name. Try to select some descriptive words that you think others may not know about you.

4. A turning point is a place in a story where the action moves toward a certain conclusion. What is the turning point in Bob's story? Suppose Mr. Drew had truly appreciated Bob's story and had encouraged him to write more. Rewrite this story with a sensitive, responsive Mr. Drew. How would this new character have affected the outcome of your story?

5. Write a journal, diary, play or short book about your life. Highlight those incidents that had the most impact upon you. Be sure to include your relation-

ships with parents, siblings, peers, influential teachers, other influential adults and relatives.

6. Paul Simon and Art Garfunkel wrote a song entitled, *I Am A Rock* (1965, 1972). How does this song tell the story of Bob's life? How is Bob like the person singing this song? Write another stanza for this song, pretending it is Bob's story.

7. As Jennie was sitting in the counselor's office facing Bob Johnson, she was reminded of a childhood game. In pairs with one of you pretending to be Bob and the other Jennie, make a list of "B" words to describe Bob. Do the same for "J" words to describe Jennie. Predict how the lists might be different.

Now, as a pair, compare the two lists. How are they alike? How are they different? List all the ways that Jenny and Bob are alike and all the ways that they are different.

8. Make a list of Bob's positive attributes. Using this list of attributes, write a cinquain (5-line stanza) describing Bob.

Analyses of Biographies

Read biographies of disadvantaged gifted kids who become successful adults. Analyze how they emerged from their economic disadvantage. Survey the analyses done by other students in your class. Are there common themes in these biographies that can help disadvantaged students?

Interviewing

On tape, interview successful gifted adults who had cultural or economic disadvantage. Ask about their family, school, friends and church influences. Listen to the tapes in class and analyze the most important impacts of their childhoods.

Increasing Sensitivity

1. Middle school is a time when conformity is a very high priority for most adolescents. Very few people are comfortable being different. Even those who claim to enjoy being different are often searching for a way to be recognized and fit into a group of friends. Brainstorm a list of things young people might do to try to fit in and be accepted by a peer group. Before you begin, make a list of some of the groups that exist in your school. Now list behaviors that would help one fit into the various groups.

Jennie made a list of her own to help her fit in with the cheerleaders. She felt she was not being accepted by them because she was too smart, and that if she hid her intelligence, maybe they would accept her. Take a look at Jennie's list and see if there are others you could add. Think of yourself or someone in your class, and see if there are some behaviors that could be classified by some as "nerdy." How did making this list help Jennie? Was it a solution to her problem? Why or why not?

2. Often it is difficult to recognize and deal with one's problems. Sometimes people choose not to

deal with a problem. There are many ways that people escape dealing with problems, some more positive ways than others. Brainstorm a list of ways to escape dealing with problems.

a. Which ways have you or people you have known tried?
b. Which ways are most effective for you?
c. Are some ways more acceptable than others?
d. Are some harmful to you or others?
e. Is there a way to take a method of escape and turn it into something positive for yourself or others?

Creative Playing

Divide your group in half. This is a game based on the Parker Bros. game, *Encore (1989)*. The object is to be the last team to think of a song lyric with a certain word in it. For a word to count, you must think of eight words in the lyric with one of the eight being the word you need. An example would be to think of a lyric with the word **star** in it. An acceptable answer would be "twinkle, twinkle little **star**. How I wonder what ..." The opposing team would sing, "When you wish upon a **star**, makes no..." The first team would then need to think of another song, "Oh, say does that **star**-spangled banner yet wave, ..." Now it's back to the second team and so forth until one team cannot think of one. The last team to think of one gets a point. Play this game with the following words:

Lonely, alone, sad, empty, friends, tears, cry, different, misery, dark, solitary

After playing the game, choose a song (either one that was used in the game or another one you know) whose lyrics deal with being alone and talk about the following questions:

1. In the song, is being alone a sad thing?
2. How does the person in the song feel about being alone?
3. Are there times when being alone is okay, even good?
4. How do different people deal with being alone?
5. Do you think that most people feel alone at some time?
6. Is there comfort in knowing most people experience loneliness?
7. Do you think that's what Mr. Jackson hoped Jennie would learn from talking with Bob? Explain.

Research

Not all gifted people make positive contributions to society. Make a list of infamous people who could have been considered gifted. Make a list of categories of people who might be gifted but who are using their talents in socially unacceptable ways. (Example would be a creative and successful bank robber or Hitler.)

Creative Drama

Have two people play the roles of Jennie and Bob. The setting is Mr. Jackson's office. Re-create the scene in the office with three different outcomes. Which of your endings was the most far-fetched or unrealistic? Why? Do you feel the author's ending was a good one? Was it realistic? Why or why not?

YOUR TIME WILL COME

Eric Rimm, Age 15

DISCUSSION QUESTIONS

1. Have you ever had difficulty communicating abstract ideas to other people? If you had the difficulty, was it related to your specialized knowledge or to your lack of communication skills?

2. This extraordinarily gifted child felt as if he was a disappointment to his father. Have you ever felt that you were a disappointment to either of your parents? If so, what are your perceptions of the reasons they felt disappointed in you? Were lack of social or communication skills ever a reason for their disappointment?

3. Have any of you been able to make big improvements in communication skills? What or who influenced your improvement in communication?

4. The boy in Eric's story had problems with oral communication. Do any of you write much better than you speak or vice-versa? What do you think has caused the great differential in skills between

your oral and written communication? How can you improve in your area of weakness?

PROJECTS AND ACTIVITIES

Survey

Eric's imaginary story about an extraordinarily gifted child who invented a time machine exaggerates a "nerd or geek" stereotype that has often existed about very gifted children. Do a survey of very gifted students in your school. Try to determine what percentage have problems communicating with others. Analyze the results by gender. In conducting the survey, also ask about the extent of students' interests in computers. Does the stereotype fit for some students in your school? Discuss with your classmates.

Analysis of Literature

Make a list of science fiction books that include time machines. Is that a popular theme? Survey the research literature to determine if people are doing any serious research on time machines or variations thereof. Brainstorm to develop a list of all the possible kinds of time machines that could be invented. After brainstorming, evaluate which ones would have potential value for our society.

Role-Play

Role-play communication of a very abstract idea to your class. Choose something that you believe that most of the class has had little exposure to. It may be in science, math, art, business, music or in any area where you have more specialized knowledge. Get feedback from the class on the quality of your communication and on whether they had sufficient background to understand your presentation.

Creative Writing

Make up your own science fiction story about a time machine and share it with your class.

MY CAT'S NAME IS EINSTEIN

DISCUSSION QUESTIONS

1. Do you know any students who have a reputation for being a "genius" or "brilliant?" If so, do you think it causes the student to feel pressured, to feel embarrassed or to feel good about their label? What are the student's characteristics which have fostered this reputation? How do students respond to "extreme" labeling?

2. What does the term "genius" mean to you?

3. Do you know any students in special education who are made fun of or teased by other kids? Do they know you well enough to share their feelings with you? If so, don't mention names, but share with your classmates the feelings these kids experience when being teased.

4. How do you think John felt about the mixture of labels used to describe him (e.g., retaard, crazy, genius, Einstein)?

5. If you were Cindy, would you want to get to know someone who had the very mixed-up reputation that John had? How would you describe Cindy's character? Would you like to have her as a friend?

6. Have you ever felt pressured to live up to a level of intelligence above which you think you're capable? Describe your feelings and think about what you've said to your friends, parents or teachers? Were you angry, sad, or did you make up excuses?

7. Have you ever befriended someone in a class for emotionally disturbed students? Don't mention their names, but tell about your experiences.

8. How else could John have coped with the teasing he got when he was at Gino's?

9. Why do you think John saw so many teachers as treating him in negative ways?

10. What special role did John's cat, Einstein, play for him? Have you ever had a pet in a very close, special relationship to you? Why are pets sometimes more effective than people for special relationships?

PROJECTS AND ACTIVITIES

Increasing Sensitivity

1. Suppose two students have exchanged places and a substitute teacher arrives on the scene unaware of the switch. The teacher has left a note that child A is to be the helper for the sub because he is extremely responsible, very capable and a model student. Because of the switch, the child who is now in child A's seat is a discipline problem, uses little effort in his daily work and rarely completes assignments. In elementary school, however, he was a quick learner and an early reader.

Come up with as many possible situations as you can think of for how this day might unfold.

What insights does this provide us with about how labeling can be a damaging thing to do?

2. Identification of gifted students is a problem that many school systems find difficult to address. Does your school identify and label gifted students? If so, what do you believe are the criteria it uses? How early in the school years are children identified?

If your school doesn't identify gifted, what criteria do you think they should use to identify students? From this discussion, make a list of possible criteria one could use for identifying gifted students.

Consider the following types of giftedness: academic, intellectual, creative, leadership, and artistic.

What did you learn about labeling gifted students by looking at criteria for identification? What did you learn about labels, in general? How can these labels influence behaviors?

3. People's attitudes and expectations can influence behaviors. How did Mrs. Steven's attitude toward John make him feel about himself?

The reader doesn't really have any background information about John's placement in the emotionally disturbed classroom. Give evidence to support each of the following possibilities:

a. John is emotionally disturbed.
b. John's **gifted** behaviors have been mistakenly labeled as **disturbed** behaviors.
c. John was labeled as gifted at a very young age. He did not understand his own giftedness. When work became more difficult for him and he had to use effort, he **felt** he was dumb. No one was able to help him with his frustrations, so he began acting out socially unacceptable behaviors.

Research

Interview special education teachers to find out the definitions of special education classes in your school. Find the criteria used for special education placement and decide as a group if students identified as gifted could also be identified for special education. If students identified as gifted are in special education, which label are they most frequently known for?

Analysis of Literature

1. Have each person in the class read a biography of a person classified as a "genius" or at least extraordinarily brilliant. Discuss the childhood and schooling of these brilliant persons. Decide if any of them might have been classified for special education programs in their time if such programs had existed. Discuss how they overcame their special educational problems if they had them.

2. In some stories, popular kids have not had good values. In this story Cindy is both popular and is kind and has excellent character. In analyzing the biographies that the class has read, were there some "brilliant" persons who also managed to be well accepted by their peers as teenagers? Discuss and describe people's characteristics who are able to combine peer acceptance with creativity and intellectual integrity. Is that a difficult combination? How does acceptance depend somewhat on the school they attend?

3. Read the biography of a famous person whom you believe was probably gifted. For this activity, select a person who was not appreciated by society until some later point in his life. Some people that you might consider would be Einstein, Helen Keller, or Worfgang Amadeus Mozart, to name just a few.

Brainstorm other names to add to this list. When you have completed your biographical research, dress up like this person and tell your group about the person you studied. Be sure you tell how you were mislabeled or misunderstood.

Debate

Form two teams, pro and con, for the purpose of debating the following issues:

1. Gifted kids should be labeled.
2. Gifted kids should be labeled, but not until fourth grade.
3. Identify gifted behaviors rather than label gifted people.
4. It is better to "misidentify" someone as gifted than to not identify them at all.

THE SKY'S MY LIMIT

Sara Franing, Age 14

DISCUSSION QUESTIONS

1. Do you ever feel as expansive as Sara did in this poem? Have you had the sense that the whole world is open to you? What kinds of situations encourage your feelings of limitlessness?

2. All of us have limits. Limits may refer to intelligence, to material possessions, to finances, to talents, or to sensitivities, etc. Talk about how you find your personal limitations as well as how you can best explore your potential abilities in various domains; for example, intellectual, artistic, physical, etc.

PROJECTS AND ACTIVITIES

Setting Goals

Make up a plan for exploring a limit in one area of interest or ability. For example, it could be a study plan, a physical exercise plan, etc. Your plan should include a long-term goal, short-term objectives, the activities or practices you will engage in, the time frame for activities and a means of evaluating your attainment of both short-term objectives and your long-term goal.

Follow your plan and determine if your goal was realistic. Can you accomplish more or less than what you planned? What enabled you to accomplish your objectives and/or goal? What prevented you or limited you in your accomplishment?

Discuss your plans with your class at intervals so that you may be able to give each other feedback, encouragement and suggestions.

NO MOTHER, NO FATHER

DISCUSSION QUESTIONS

1. Do you know anyone who comes from a family environment such as Anna's where it is indeed difficult for her to feel good about living at home? Don't mention names, but discuss situations and alternatives to coping with a difficult family situation.

2. Do you think Anna will be successful in college? Do you know any other students who graduated early? Were they successful? What are the advantages and disadvantages of early graduation?

3. Most students who have attempted suicide will not try again and are thankful that they stopped before it was too late. Students who have committed suicide are often found in situations where one can tell they wanted to stop themselves, but changed their minds too late. Have you known students who have attempted suicide? In your experience, were the students that you know convinced never to try again? Why do you think this happens?

4. Do you know any students whose mother or father died? How did that seem to affect them? How can you be of help to friends who have only one parent and may have lost the other through death or divorce or some other circumstance?

5. Have you ever had a very close friend that you share almost everything with? Has that friend stayed loyal to you? Has that friend preserved your privacy? Talk about the advantages and disadvantages of confiding in close friends.

PROJECTS AND ACTIVITIES

Family Tree

Anna Washington had no ties with her birth heritage and although her adopted father apparently loved her, she felt deceived by him because he had never told her he was not her birth father. She had neither mother nor father who was genetically related to her. That left her with a feeling of unconnectedness.

Map your own family tree as far back as you can, including your family as either genetically related or related by adoption. Discuss your family trees and your feelings in regard to genetic or adoptive family relationships. Also discuss the issues that stepparents and stepchildren feel.

Survey

Survey your class to determine the percentage of students who live with both parents, adopted parents, stepparents or single parents. What is typical for your class? Research what is typical in the United States today.

How does your school compare to typical kids? How is what is typical likely to affect students who live in homes with atypical parenting styles? What do you project for future families as far as family styles? You may want to check the library for updated data on typical family information.

Research

Review the research on early entrance to college. Have students make reports on the available programs for early entrance to college and the circumstances under which such early entrance is advisable.

Try to arrange to interview, in person, by telephone or letter, students who have entered college early. Were they pleased or disappointed with their decision?

Creative Writing

Pretend you are in Katie's situation. Brainstorm possible plans for Anna Washington's problems. Select a different plan for Anna and rewrite the ending to the story as if Anna had followed the plan you suggested.

Increasing Sensitivity

1. Educators are becoming more aware of the fact that minority students are often disadvantaged because of their backgrounds. There is evidence to support that lower test grades might be partially due to cultural differences that cause minority students to answer questions differently than caucasian students. Test makers are trying to remove questions that might disadvantage minority students. Many school

districts are working to improve minority student achievement.

Make a list of ways that a minority student might be disadvantaged in a suburban middle or high school.

Make a list of ways that a minority student might be disadvantaged in an inner city school where minorities are the majority.

Are there some problems that appear on both lists that come from being a minority student regardless of the setting?

Are there some problems that appear on one list or the other that seem to arise from the setting?

2. The author of the story gives the reader some idea of what life is like in both Katie's and Anna's homes. Write a paragraph describing life at Anna's. Write another paragraph describing life at Katie's.

Both girls are being raised in economically disadvantaged homes. What differences do you see in the two environments? Which of the two girls do you believe is the more fortunate? Why?

Without a supportive home, even very gifted students will have difficulty being achievers. What problems did Anna need to deal with at home that probably resulted from the family's economic situation? She also came from a home where no one had previously gone to college. How can that disadvantage her?

Setting Goals

1. How does setting a goal for yourself help you to achieve? Think of some goals you have set for yourself. Have you ever set unrealistic goals, ones that were impossible or almost impossible for you to reach?

How did these goals make you feel? Were the goals so impossible that they actually prevented you from trying? Did your inability to reach your goals influence how you felt about yourself?

How could you apply what you have just learned from your own frustrations to how a minority student might feel about trying to go to college?

Because of Katie's socio/economic position, many things will be working against her. In spite of these things, what is working in her favor? Would you predict that she will go to college?

2. Over the next two-week period, practice setting some attainable goals. Make a chart showing a two-week period. In this calendar or chart, choose a short-term goal that you would like to reach **each** day. Choose a slightly more long-range goal for the third day, a longer one for one week, another for 10 days, and a long-range goal for the last day of the two-week chart.

Work to set goals that will need some effort on your part (in other words, not something that is automatic for you), but that is possible for you to accomplish. These can pertain to your school or home life.

Keep a log that you write in at the end of each day, telling how you are doing with your daily goals and how you are feeling about work toward your longer-range goals.

How do you feel as you reach a goal? What pressure are you experiencing? What are your positive and negative feelings about the goals themselves and the reaching of the goals? How are you feeling about yourself as a person? What are your feelings of self-worth? Are they affected by setting and attaining goals? Are family members, friends, and teachers influencing how you are feeling about yourself relative to the accomplishing of your goals? Are you receiving encouragement from others?

If you could use encouragement from others but are not getting it, do you know how or where to look for this encouragement? Is it easier to attain your goals and increase your self-esteem if you have support from others? How did setting goals and the support from Katie and the school psychologist turn around Anna's life?

Analysis of a Movie

Stand and Deliver (1987) is an excellent movie showing the difficulties that minority or economically disadvantaged students face beyond those faced by many bright students. After viewing this movie, discuss the following questions with your group:

1. What were some of the problems these students faced in their attempt to get to class and study for the advanced placement test that are not typically faced by middle class students?

2. What might be some possible explanations for the teacher's commitment, drive, and energy?

3. Having an achieving role model is often important in the successful accomplishments of others. Give some examples of how the teacher served this role.

4. Would you like to have this teacher for your teacher? Why or why not?

5. An additional barrier that minority students face is the biased assessment of their intelligence. How did the movie illustrate and deal with this problem?

CONGRATULATIONS, MS. SMITHERSTEEN, YOU'VE PROVEN AMY ISN'T GIFTED

DISCUSSION QUESTIONS

1. Have you ever experienced the frustration of persons having expectations for you that you believe are inaccurate? What have you done about such a problem? Was there anything else that you believe Amy or her mother could have done?

2. Have you known students who surprised you by unusual performance in school activities, either better or worse? What usually causes their unusual performance? What kinds of events tend to cause kids to either dramatically improve or do especially poorly?

3. When classes are grouped homogeneously, for example, all the gifted kids in the same class, what ways of assigning grades do you think would be fair? How does your school treat grading for special ability groups?

4. How do grades affect your motivation? Has that been different for you in some grades and/or subjects?

5. How do you feel about teachers announcing grades in class or posting them where others may see them?

PROJECTS AND ACTIVITIES

Role-Play

Role-play a discussion on grading between students who are in accelerated classes and those who are in average classes where the grading criteria are different. If the accelerated students could only earn *A*s and *B*s and the average students could earn no *A*s, argue those points. Imagine different possible arrangements and role-play the potential differences in point of view.

Research

Interview adults of various ages and ask them about the grading systems used when they were in school. Try to analyze whether some systems were more commonly used at different time periods, different geographic locations, or public versus private schools.

Design an ideal grading system that you believe would best motivate students. Discuss in class to see if your class can reach consensus on the best system.

Analogies

Try the following analogies for Ms. Smithersteen, Mrs. Robertson, and Amy (Davis, 1986, 1983):

Ms. Smithersteen is like

a tree because ____________
an apple because ____________
an earthquake because ____________
a slipper because ____________
a smile because ____________
a vacation because ____________
a gavel because ____________
a clock because ____________
a lagoon because ____________
a lion because ____________

Now repeat these for Mrs. Robertson and Amy. How does use of these analogies help one to see these characters in a different light?

Debate

Divide the group in half to form two debate teams. One team will research the position that accelerated, honors, advanced placement-type courses should receive some sort of weighted grade. They should find as many arguments in support of this position as they can. The researchers should keep track of authors, articles, and research study details to strengthen their arguments.

The other team will take the opposite position; that no grading advantage should be given for more difficult courses.

Three- to four-man-debate teams should be used for the debate. Videotape the debate itself.

Which side of this issue do you think Ms. Smithersteen would support? On what are you basing this opinion?

How do you think Amy's mother, Mrs. Robertson, would feel based on her experience with Ms. Smithersteen?

What position would you take on this issue? What position has your school district taken on this issue?

After participating in this debate, how does your class feel about the issue? If your class feels differently than the district, consider preparing a videotape to use to persuade them to change their position. The whole group could do additional research on the same side of this issue to prepare for their presentation to district administration.

Increasing Sensitivity

What is an advocate? How does someone advocate for something? In what way did Mrs. Robertson serve as an advocate for Amy? Mrs. Robertson tried very hard to be a positive advocate. What were some of the things she tried to do to keep a positive position in her advocacy role? How did Amy feel about her mother's actions? Should parents discuss these types of issues with their children before they meet with the teacher?

Under what conditions would you want a parent to serve as an advocate for you? Have you ever tried to advocate for yourself? When might that work?

Comparisons in Literature

Read the story, *The Gift*, by Joseph Wayman of Houston, Texas, aloud in class. (Story follows.)

What do you think the gift might have been? What gradually became of the gift? What happened to the little girl when no one was excited about her gift? How long did it take for the little girl to get discouraged?

Now read Lisa Lovance's poem, *The Gift*, again. How do the story, *The Gift*, and the poem, *The Gift*, relate to the Ms. Smithersteen story? What do you think could happen to Amy's gift if she had a second year in a classroom like Ms. Smithersteen's? Compare this story to Lisa's poem, *The Gift*.

What is the concern of all of these authors? In your own years in school, have you seen students get discouraged? What types of behaviors have they exhibited that lead you to believe that they are no longer achieving up to their potential? Would it be easy for teachers to not see these students as being gifted?

THE GIFT*

by Joseph Wayman

Once there was a little girl who went to school. She wasn't very big, but she was a very special little girl because she had a gift. Yes, this little girl had a very special gift...a gift all her own and unlike anyone else's in the entire world.

One day when the sun was shining and everything seemed bright and happy the little girl decided it was a perfect time to show her gift to her teacher. Her teacher seemed very tall and sometimes far away and very busy. But the little girl decided that it was very important for the teacher to see her gift. She waited until the teacher seemed to be a little less busy and then she said, "Teacher, look. I want to show you my gift." The teacher looked very surprised. She smiled and said, "Isn't that nice. But you really shouldn't have your gift in school--school is a place where we learn about other kinds of things." And she told the little girl to put her gift away and get busy on her times tables and her punctuation marks.

The little girl felt a bit sad, and when she looked at her gift it didn't seem quite so bright and colorful as it had a few minutes before. But she put the gift away and tried to keep her mind on 2x2, 3x3, 6x6.

*Used with the permission of Joseph Wayman

But very soon she was thinking about her gift again. "I know what I'll do," she thought, "I'll show my gift to the principal...he will think it is beautiful." She took her gift out of the desk and slipped out of the room.

When she saw the principal she lifted her gift high into the air for him to see..."What are you doing in the hall? Yes, yes," he said, "your gift is very nice but you get back to class now. Put that gift away and go to work on your times tables and punctuation marks."

Now the little girl felt very sad...and her gift looked sort of faded and shabby. "I'll bet the librarian would like to see my gift," she thought. And with lots of hope she hurried to the library. Standing on tip-toe she held her worn and torn gift way up for the librarian to see. The librarian's eyes went up in surprise and a cross look clouded her eyes. "Don't you know that gifts don't belong in the library?" she said. "You put it away, better still, take it home with you and keep it there. Now, go back to your classroom. You will soon be so far behind that you will never catch up!"

The little girl held her gift tightly in her arms. It had all but faded away by now and her tears dropped from her cheeks and landed, plop, plop, on the dull gray wrapping paper which had been so bright and pretty such a short time before.

With one faint hope left, she waited till the final bell of the day rang and she ran to her friends. As they came down the hall she held her gift--so worn and torn--out for them to see. Their laughter over-shadowed the last hope she had. "Why did you bring that ol' gift to school?" they wanted to know. "You know it doesn't belong here!"

The little girl stood all by herself in that long empty hallway and the sound of the doors clanging shut echoed through the deserted building. She looked down at her gift, now so shabby and drab that there was no color left in it at all.

Sadly she walked back into the empty classroom. She stuffed her gift way down in the bottom of her desk under all the books and old multiplication papers where no one would see it. It will just have to stay here, she thought, cause no one wants to see it or have it at school.

She never got it out again...and after several years she forgot she had ever had such a wonderful gift. But it didn't matter any more, her friends didn't laugh and her teachers were happy with her multiplication tables.

BROTHERS AND SISTERS

DISCUSSION QUESTIONS

1. Describe situations where you may have felt inadequate because a brother or sister did something better than you or where your sister or brother may have felt badly because you accomplished something that he or she hadn't.

2. How can you best cope with jealous feelings that you may have about sisters, brothers or friends? Do you find you can admit these feelings of jealousy or do you sometimes use those feelings as an excuse to avoid an activity or responsibility?

3. Discuss the rules of competition in several sports. Now generalize these rules to the classroom and to schoolwork. Talk about the ways in which applying the rules of good sportsmanship to learning can help to improve a student's attitude about school achievement.

4. Have you participated in any types of cooperative group learning such as those in the

Johns Hopkins Team Learning Project (Slavin, 1980)? If not, perhaps your class could experience or observe a cooperative group situation. An easy beginning activity might be a group of four learning a list of spelling words. Discuss your feelings and reactions to this type of learning. How do cooperative groups differ from other methods in their approach to competition? How does this compare to real world situations?

5. Why do you think Drew got up and left Allison's house so suddenly? Describe feelings that you may have when a friend gets better grades than you and you're disappointed in your own performance. What do you do?

6. Is it possible to not have feelings about competition in our society? How can feelings of competition help us and how can they hurt us? Do students often have feelings about competition that they do not acknowledge or even deny?

PROJECTS AND ACTIVITIES

Interviewing

1. Interview your parents, grandparents, aunts and/or uncles to ask about how they got along with their siblings. Tape the interviews and see if you can interpret jealous feelings that they may admit to and jealous feelings they may not admit having felt. How have they coped with those feelings? Do they continue to have problems dealing with jealously as adults? Bring this information into class for discussion but don't mention names or relationships. During the discussion, students may refer to family members as **this** person or **this** relationship, thus preserving confidentiality. Do not have them bring actual tapes into class.

2. Think of some families that you know where siblings have all been successful in the same areas (i.e. sports, music, academics.) See if you can interview the children and parents to see how they have dealt with competition and with more than one child who was interested in the same interest area.

Apparently, Allison's younger sister was experiencing feelings similar to Drew's, but had never expressed them. What might you predict will come out of their family discussion about Drew that will benefit Janet? What do you think could have contributed to Allison's attitude about school and competition with siblings being different from Janet's?

Did you get any help in answering this question from the interviews you did?

Analysis

Sometimes members in a family are informally labeled by other family members. One child may be considered the "scholar", another the "jock", a third the "social" one and a fourth the "creative" or "artistic" one. Analyze the siblings of all class members to see if they have received informal labels. Don't use names to preserve confidentiality. Total the numbers on the board to determine the proportion of each category. Then discuss how competition causes the informal labeling. Do you think this informal labeling is beneficial or detrimental to children's development?

Analysis of Literature

Read biographies of the childhoods of eminent persons with attention to the effect on sisters and brothers. Discuss in class the accomplishments and responses of other family members to the success of other family members. Did sibling rivalry seem to have an effect on other siblings or did there tend to be "whole smart families?"

Role-Play

Allison was imagining the conversation she would have about her lessons in competition with her boyfriend. What do you think she might say? How do you think her friend would respond? Role-play the conversation you might have with a friend who you sensed was feeling competition with you. Have students in the class role-play different relationships, for example, sisters, sister/brother, brothers, cousins, or girlfriend/boyfriend. Discuss the role-plays after all are over. Were some relationships harder to act out than others? Why?

Increasing Sensitivity to Competition

1. Find a list of frequently misspelled words. Have an old-fashioned spelling bee where you repeat the word, spell it, and then re-state the word. If you make an error, you sit down. Discuss how you felt about the spelling bee.

Now make three lists of words -- one list with the most difficult words (worth 20 points), one with medium difficulty (worth 10 points), and one with easier words (worth 5 points). Divide the group into two teams. Now have a spelling bee where each person gets to choose a point value word and a total team score is kept. The first team to reach 500 points wins. Compare and contrast how you felt with this type of spelling bee. Which was more fun?

Which was more embarrassing? Which was more fair? How was the competition different?

Invent a spelling game that incorporates competition for each player to improve himself but does not have competition with others. Compare all of the games. How did they make you feel?

2. Use this technique to brainstorm the following issue:

> Make a list of slogans, sayings, commercials, signs that deal with competition, especially focusing on those that would lead one to believe it's important to be the best, number one, first. How does society contribute to Drew's feelings of competition with his brother?

Do commercials and other media sources contribute to the feeling that if you are not #1 you have failed? How can we learn to deal with these influences? A current army song says "Be all that you can be -- in the army." How does this song differ from the list you compiled?

3. What do you suppose the parents meant when they said "You can have a whole smart family?" Think of some times when you or someone you knew felt in competition with a sibling. What were the circumstances? How did you or the sibling feel about the situation? Why do you think you felt this way? Have you ever felt in competition with good friends? How did it make you feel? Did it cause you to not do your personal best?

One way adults sometimes try to deal with this competition is to tell you that it is okay if you are not as good as someone else and then try to help you find something where you can be better than your sibling or friend or be "the best" in a different interest area. What message is this giving to you? Why can this lead to a problem like Drew's and Janet's? How can this lead a person to underachieve or do less than his personal best?

4. *Hoosiers (1986), Breaking Away (1979)*, and *Chariots of Fire* (1981) are all movies about the competition in sports. View one or all of them and discuss the theme in them. Again try to understand how fear of failure could prevent a person from trying at all or could prevent a person from putting forth his best effort.

Creative Writing

1. Break into groups of three or four. Read several of Aesop's Fables (1927), looking for some that are about competition. Select one to act out for the class. Try to have each group choose a different story. Talk about the different types of competition in these stories and how the stories might help one to understand how competition is in so many areas of our lives. Write you own fable that illustrates one type of competition.

2. Choose one of the following books. Read it and write a book report discussing the theme of competition in it:

A Separate Peace - John Knowles (1960)
Lord of the Flies - William Golding (1954)
Sons from Afar - Cynthia Voight (1987)

Analysis of a Film

View the movie, *The Competition (1980)*. The character played by Amy Irving is faced with some difficult choices during a piano competition. Did you predict what choice she would make? Can you predict what Richard Dreyfus's character's reaction would be if he were to win or lose?

Did you like the ending of the movie? Was it believable? What did each of the characters learn from his/her experience?

REAL LIFE: A BOY WHO DOESN'T CARE

Bradley Jones, Age 14

DISCUSSION QUESTIONS

1. Why do you think Brad didn't do all his homework? Do you think that Brad knew why he wasn't doing his homework? Have you ever found yourself avoiding assignments? Under what circumstances did you not do your work? Did you understand why you were not doing your homework?

2. What do you think underachievement means? Can gifted students also be underachievers? Do you know some students who are underachievers? Don't mention names, but describe why you think they are underachievers?

3. Do you believe that there is such a thing as overachievement? Can people achieve more than what they are capable of or only to the top of their abilities? What are the characteristics of high achievers?

4. Do you think that Brad felt very good about himself while he was underachieving?

5. Brad's writing is very creative. He does a fine job of sharing his feelings and providing a very good description of his environment. Could his creativity have interfered with his achievement? How could that happen? What are the problems involved for "real world" productive creativity? Read the article, *Marching to the Beat of a Different Drummer* (Rimm, 1987a). Does that give you any insight into underachieving creative students?

PROJECTS AND ACTIVITIES

Increasing Sensitivity

1. Make a list of adjectives to describe the boy in the story. When you look at your list, try to find some pairs of words that are opposites or close to opposites. Do you have some pairs such as "cares" and "indifferent," "bored" and "it'd be great to get "*B*s", and "arrogant" and "lacking confidence?" What do these pairs of words tell you about the complex nature of the boy's underachievement problem?

2. Caring about someone can be positive, but it is not always enough. In this story the boy hears that his parents care, but it does not make any difference to him. He, in fact, finds it irritating that they do. Teachers and the school also seem to be involved but have not found a way to change the boy's underachievement pattern. The parents had sought help when they took the boy to a psychologist in Wisconsin. By the end of the story, do you predict that the boy will begin achieving? If you predict that he will, on what are you basing this prediction? Why is it not enough for others to be feeling that the boy needs to achieve? At the end of the story, why is it significant that the fish is not watching?

3. Design a program that might help an underachieving gifted student you know. Don't mention the student, but discuss with your class how

you think you could help the student. Talk about what you think the student you know may be feeling.

Research

Read books or articles about underachievement or listen to tapes. (Rimm, 1984, 1986, 1987, 1989) Are there things you can learn that will help you to avoid being an underachiever in high school and college? Discuss in class the risks for underachievement among gifted students.

LONELINESS

Bradley Jones, Age 14

DISCUSSION QUESTIONS

1. Have you ever experienced complete aloneness for any length of time? How did it affect you? Compare that to Brad's experience.

2. How is the loneliness which Brad feels similar to and different from the aloneness that Lisa Lovance, Andrew Rubinstein and Shalicia Johnson expressed in their poems or the aloneness that Eric Rimm described in his story? What do these have in common and how are they different?

3. Brad's alone time was a deeply religious experience for him. Have any of you felt a deeply religious experience? Share with the class your experience and how it affected you.

PROJECTS AND ACTIVITIES

Creative Writing

Write in poetry or prose about an experience with loneliness or aloneness. Share it with your class and discuss the similarities and differences in the experiences of your classmates.

Increasing Sensitivity

Brainstorm and then plan an individual experience where you may have some sense of aloneness. Share your experiences afterward with your class. How did it seem similar or different from Brad's, Lisa's, Shalicia's or Andrew's?

TO BE STRONG

DISCUSSION QUESTIONS

1. Have you ever felt caught between being accepted by the "popular crowd" and your own personal values? Describe some experiences.

2. Were you ever at a party where you felt excited about "finally fitting in," although you knew that your parents wouldn't approve of your being there?

3. What main differences are there between the social life you believe your parents were exposed to and the social experiences of your friends?

4. What are the differences among the social experiences of various groups of students in your school?

5. How do social values affect school achievement of students and how do these social values affect their future careers?

6. Do you think that Kaaren handled her situation well? What other solutions could she have tried?

7. How do you feel about Kaaren's friend, Lisa? Discuss appropriate responsibilities of friendship. How much is too much control between friends?

8. Do you think Josh was taking advantage of Kaaren from the start? What responsibilities go with guys' sexual advances and girls' sexual involvement or advances?

9. How important is your personal independence? How effective is peer pressure on you? On others?

10. How does friendship differ from popularity?

PROJECTS AND ACTIVITIES

Analysis

Analyze the friendship groups within your grade. Draw a sociogram to represent the leadership and friendship relations of these groups. List the priority values and activities of each friendship group. Are there differences and similarities among groups?

Role-play the perspectives of persons in the various groups. Defend your values and activities. Does this increase your understanding of students in different groups?

Interviewing

Interview adults who are approximately ten, twenty, thirty, forty and fifty years older than you. Ask them about social relations, values, activities and problems of their generation. Analyze, in writing or discussion in class, the similarities and differences among generations. How do your comparisons over time affect how you feel about your present social life?

Project to the future for your children. What do you think their social lives will be like? What do all generations have in common?

Analysis of Literature

Read fiction about teenagers written during various time periods. Does the fiction reflect the different values and norms of the time periods? Are there similarities within books that may reflect similarities in adolescent development over time? Was intellectual achievement valued differently during various time periods?

Learning About Compromises

What is a compromise? Look up the dictionary definition.

Make a list of some famous compromises that have taken place in the history of our country. Choose one of them and make a list of the issues that existed on each side **before** a compromise was reached. What did each side give up in order to reach an agreeable compromise?

Have someone in your group look up Henry Clay to see why he was called "The Great Compromiser." Share your reports with your group.

What are some benefits of compromising? Why is it important to learn when a person needs to compromise? What are some situations in your family or with your friends, when you felt it was important to compromise?

What are some times when you hope you will be strong and independent enough not to compromise? Are there some things you have already decided not to compromise? When Kaaren listened to the "little voice inside her head," it told her not to "compromise her integrity." What do you think this means? By not compromising, what has Lisa gained?

Increasing Sensitivity

1. Blind Walk. For this activity, you will need to work with a partner. Each person will need a piece of dark material to tie around the head as a blindfold. No light should show through the material. The partner without the blindfold will lead the blindfolded person on a 10-minute walk. The blindfolded person should hold the forearm of the person who is leading. The leader will give as many auditory directions as possible, like "you will be coming to a doorway in about five steps. Be careful because after going through the doorway, there are two steps down." The leader should take the person to several places where the blind person should be given instructions to try to do something like make a phone call from a pay booth or get a soda from the vending machine. After ten minutes, reverse positions so that the blind person is now the leader.

Talk about the experience. How did it feel to be the guide? What was it like to be the blind person? Which position was easier for you? Did you trust the person right away, or did it take some time? What if the person you trusted led you into a wall? What would happen to the trust? Would it take a while to re-establish the trust?

How could you apply what you learned from the experience to the relationship between Kaaren and her parents? Is "trust" an issue in your family? How could you spoil the trust that your parents have in you? Have you had an experience where you spoiled the trust? Are you able to earn the trust back? Will it be the same?

2. Read the story *Sneetches* from the book *Sneetches and Other Stories* (1961) by Dr. Suess. What is the theme of this story? Dr. Suess wrote this as a children's story, but it obviously has a message for everyone. What does one give up in order to be a part of the "group?" What did Lisa give up or come close to giving up to be "popular?"

Where do drugs and alcohol fit into your school's social scene? Do you believe or are there those who would like you to believe that drugs and alcohol are necessary to be in the "in-crowd?" Do drug education and programs make it any easier to resist the pressures that some people feel exist?

Creative Writing

1. One thing that we obviously have no control over but that can influence our lives is our birth order. Have you ever wished that you were not the oldest, the baby of the family, the only child, that you had a sister instead of a brother, that you were not the only boy in a household of girls or that you could be an only child? Each position in the family has its unique privileges and disadvantages.

Write a story where you have had the opportunity to trade places with one of your siblings. If you are an only child, you get to create a sibling or two and place yourself anywhere in the family. Your story should include what you see to be the advantages and disadvantages from your new point of view in this position in the family.

Keep in mind that Lisa's older brother, Jason, had disappointed her parents. How did Lisa, being the second child, influence her mother's reaction when she learned Lisa had lied to attend the party with Josh?

2. Try your hand at being a children's author like Dr. Suess and write a children's story pertaining to one of the issues in the story. It could be about trust, compromising, conformity or any other issue you feel is relevant to this story.

Research

Each generation of young people has its own taste in music, art and fashion. Develop a bulletin board, booklet or research project which reflects teenage taste differences in any of the three areas. Share your project with your class.

STANDING ALONE

Shalicia Johnson, Age 13

DISCUSSION QUESTIONS

1. Do you think Shalicia feels lonely or comfortable in her aloneness?

2. What kind of "war zone" do you think Shalicia is referring to?

3. How is Shalicia's poem similar to Brad's story on loneliness? How is it different?

4. How do you feel about doing things alone? How are lonely and alone similar and how are they different?

5. What kinds of experiences do you prefer to have alone?

6. What kinds of experiences make you feel uncomfortable about being alone?

PROJECTS AND ACTIVITIES

Analysis of Literature

Find other poems and stories written about aloneness or loneliness. Read them aloud to your class and discuss the differences and similarities in the ways in which poets and authors describe these experiences.

Creative Writing

Write a poem or story on the value of aloneness. Also write a poem or story on the feelings of being part of a group. Read these aloud and talk about the advantages and disadvantages of lonely experiences and the advantages and disadvantages of group experiences. Are their individual differences in preferences for aloneness versus being in a group?

READING REFERENCES

Aesop. (1927). *Aesop's fables*. New York, NY: Harper and Rowe Publishers, Inc.

Brown, B.B., & Steinberg, L. (1989, Fall). Skirting the brain-nerd connection: How bright students save face among peers. In *Newsletter, National Center on Effective Secondary Schools*, School of Education, University of Wisconsin-Madison, *4*(2), 2-4.

Davis, G.A. (2nd Ed.). (1986, 1983). *Creativity is forever*. Dubuque, IA: Kendall/Hunt Publishing Co.

Golding, W. (1954). *Lord of the flies*. New York, NY: Capricorn.

Keirsey, D., & Bates, M. (1978). *Please understand me: Character and temperament types.* Del Mar, CA: Prometheus/Nemesis Book Co.

Knowles, J. (1960). *A separate peace.* New York, NY: Macmillan Publishing Co., Inc.

Parnes, S.J., Noller, R.B., Biondi, A.M. (1976). *Guide to creative action - Revised edition of creative behavior guidebook*. New York, NY: Charles Scribner's Sons.

*Rimm, S.B. (1984). Underachievement ... or if god had meant gifted children to run our homes, she would have created them bigger. *G/C/T*, 26-29.

Rimm, S.B. (1986). *Underachievement syndrome: Causes and cures*. Watertown, WI: Apple Publishing Company.

*Rimm, S.B. (1987a, January/February). Marching to the beat of a different drummer. *Gifted Child Today*, 2-6.

*Rimm, S.B. (1987b, November/December). Why do bright children underachieve? The pressures they feel. *Gifted Child Today, 10(53), 30-36.*

Rimm, S.B. (1987c, November/December). Is popularity worth pursuing? *Free Spirit, Vol. 1*(2), 2.

*Rimm, S.B. (1988, May/June). Popularity ends at grade 12! *Gifted Child Today, 11*(56), 42-44.

Rimm, S.B. (1990). *Gifted kids have feelings too.* Watertown, WI: Apple Publishing Company.

Rimm, S.B., Cornale, M., Manos, R., & Behrend, J. (1989). *Guidebook-Underachievement syndrome: Causes and cures*. Watertown, WI: Apple Publishing Co.

*These articles are included in the Guidebook-Underachievement Syndrome: Causes and Cures, (cited above).

Seuss, Dr. (1961). The sneetches. In *The Sneetches and Other Stories*. New York, NY: Random House, Inc.

Slavin, R.E. (1980). *Using student team learning*. Baltimore, MD: Johns-Hopkins Team Learning Project.

Voight, C. (1987). Sons from afar. New York, NY: Athenum.

AUDIO/VISUALREFERENCES

(Movies)

Breaking Away. ((1979). 100 min. Director: Peter Yates. Rated PG.

Chariots of Fire. (1981). 123 min. Director: Hugh Hudson. Rated PG.

Competition, The. (1980). 129 min. Writer/Director: Joel Oliansky. Rated PG.

Dead Poet's Society. (1989). 128 min. Writer: Tom Schulman. Rated PG.

Hoosiers. (1986). 114 min. Writer: Angelo Pizzo. Director: David Anspaugh. Rated PG.

Stand and Deliver. (1987). 105 mins. Writers: Ramon Menendez & Tom Musca. Rated PG.

(Sound Recordings)

Rimm, S.B. (1988). *Underachievement syndrome: Causes and cures*. Audio cassette 6-tape set. Watertown, WI: Educational Assessment Service, Inc.

Simon, P. (1965). I am a rock. In *Sounds of Silence*, record album, by Eclectic Music Co. Also in (1972) *Simon & Garfunkel Greatest Hits,* record album. New York, NY: Columbia Records, CBS.

(Game)

Encore. (1989). Encore (#0033) is a trademark of Parker Bros. for it's competitive singing game. Div. of Tonka Corp., Beverly, MA 01915.

(Tests)

Myers, I., Briggs, C., & Briggs, I. (1988, 1976). (*MBTI*) *The Myers-Briggs Type Indicator*. Consulting Psychologists' Press, 577 College Avenue, Palo Alto, CA 94306-1490.

Complete the order form on reverse side for additional books and cassette tapes by Sylvia B. Rimm.

BOOKS:

Gifted Kids Have Feelings Too	$15.00
Exploring Feelings A Discussion Book for Gifted Kids Have Feelings Too	15.00
How To Parent So Children Will Learn	15.00
Underachievement Syndrome: Causes and Cures	15.00
Guidebook - Underachievement Syndrome: Causes and Cures	32.00
Education of the Gifted & Talented by Gary A. Davis & Sylvia B. Rimm	39.00

TAPE SETS:

How To Parent So Children Will Learn (set of 3)	25.00
Underachievement Syndrome: Causes and Cures (set of 6)	50.00
Educating Gifted Children (set of 2)	18.00

EDUCATIONAL ASSESSMENT SERVICE, INC.
W6050 Apple Rd., Watertown, WI 53094

TO ORDER BY PHONE:
Call (414) 261-1118, 8 to 3 FAX (414) 261-6622
Monday through Friday

☐ Check enclosed payable to: Educational Assessment Service, Inc.
☐ Purchase order enclosed
☐ Charge to: ☐ VISA ☐ MasterCard

Card # ____________

Expiration Date ____

Name ______________________

Address ______________________

NO P.O. BOX PLEASE

____
SIGNATURE

City ______________ State ________ Zip ________ Phone ( ) ______________

DESCRIPTION	QUANTITY	UNIT PRICE	TOTAL PRICE

Psychology & Education of the Gifted Course	Check For Free Information ☐	Subtotal
Fourth National RIMM Underachievement Institute	Check For Free Information ☐	Shipping / Handling
		WI residents add 5% sales tax
		TOTAL

Shipping and Handling Chart:	Subtotal Amount . . . Add
$20 or less $2.00	Over $200 . . . . 5%
Over $20 to $200 . . . . 10%	Outside Continental U.S. 20%

All orders are normally shipped within 48 hours. In the event of any undue delay, you will be notified.

- Prices are subject to change without notice.
- All payments must be made through US banks or by international money order.
- Billings are NET 30 days, sorry, no C.O.D. orders.
- Orders requesting delayed billing will be held for shipment until the billing date requested.
- Our Customer Service Department must receive written notice of any problems within 30 days of receipt of your order.
- Materials returned in unusable and damaged condition will be appropriately billed.